So You're
Retired!

Mike Haskins & Clive Whichelow

summersdale

SO YOU'RE RETIRED!

Copyright © Mike Haskins and Clive Whichelow 2008

Illustrations by Ian Baker

Summersdale Publishers Ltd
46 West Street
Chichester
West Sussex
PO19 1RP
UK

www.summersdale.com

Printed and bound by Imago

ISBN: 1-84024-639-1
ISBN 13: 978-1-84024-639-1

INTRODUCTION

So you've finally done it! You've finished work! You're done! You've retired!

No one tells you what to do any more. No one tells you where to go, how to do it, how long it should take and what it's supposed to look like when it's finished. Now you are the master of your destiny, free to do whatever you like for the rest of your days!

Absolutely terrifying isn't it?

But never mind because you're free! You've left the rat race and rejoined the human race! Your life's work is complete. Or if it's not, somebody else is now having to complete it. Or maybe they're having to start again from scratch. Or maybe there's a number of people all now employed to sort out whatever it was you thought you were doing all those years in what they're calling 'a salvage operation'.

But never mind! You don't care any more!

You're free to do all those things you've always dreamt of doing. Going on cruises, going on safaris, visiting friends and family on the other side of the world, yelling at travel agents about how the hell they expect you to afford these prices on a pension.

You've got exciting new life choices: golf or bowls, painting a watercolour or painting the ceiling, rambling off or rambling on…

You know how you used to think there was nothing worth watching on TV in the evening? Well wait till you see daytime TV!

Best of all you can just sit back and take it easy – the only trouble is now you won't be getting paid for it.

Here's to a happy, healthy and fantastic retirement!

MYTHS ABOUT RETIREMENT

You can look forward to going on some exciting trips – you'll be able to get your own stairlift in a few years.

You will at last write your fabulously successful novel – well you may get to page four.

You'll have time to swim with dolphins and see the Pyramids – but not the energy unfortunately.

You'll have the time to stay in bed all morning – but not the bladder.

You'll be able to devote your time to sorting out the garden – well, you would if you hadn't concreted the whole area over two years ago.

WHAT THEY SAID ON YOUR RETIREMENT CARD AND WHAT THEY REALLY MEANT

See you again soon! = I will never see you again ever!

I envy you getting out of here! = God help you, you poor old bugger!

It won't be the same here without you! = At last we'll be able to get something done round here!

Signature only = I couldn't even be bothered to write 'Good luck'.

THINGS YOU'LL MISS
ABOUT WORK

Free heating during the winter

Free stationery supplies

 Free coffee from the drinks machine

 Providing an active contribution to the national economy – only kidding!

 Knowing what you were supposed to be doing between Monday and Friday

 Being able to go home at the end of the day

 Daydreaming about all the great things you could do once you've retired

JOBS YOU CAN OFFICIALLY APPLY FOR NOW YOU'VE RETIRED

Being Father Christmas or Mrs Claus for the local department store.

Tea boy/girl at the place where you used to work.

School crossing patrol officer (that's lollipop man/lady to you rather than the law enforcement/superhero figure you were imagining).

WHAT YOU USED TO DO VERSUS WHAT YOU'LL BE DOING NOW INSTEAD

BEFORE	NOW
Using the office computer to look up things on eBay	Using eBay to sell the office equipment that has found its way back to your house
Having to look busy occasionally whenever the boss went past	Having to look busy constantly because you're under full-time surveillance by your spouse
Feeling a bit bored and wishing you weren't at work	Feeling a bit bored and wishing you were back at work
Having a range of other people available to help sort out any problems and/or pass the blame onto	Cursing rather a lot
Phoning in sick even when you weren't that ill	Carrying on regardless no matter how terrible you feel

WHAT THEY'RE DOING AT WORK NOW YOU'RE GONE (YOU'D LIKE TO THINK)

Running round like headless chickens.

Regaling one another with stories about
the good old days when you
used to work there.

Putting up a large and elegant portrait
of you in the foyer which members of
staff glance at reverentially as they
pass by before brushing
away a little tear.

RETIRED

WHAT THEY'RE DOING AT WORK NOW YOU'RE GONE (IN REALITY)

Trying to work out what the hell it was you used to do.

Wondering why the business has suddenly become profitable after all these years.

Realising they don't have to order
anywhere near as much stationery
as they had to previously.

Providing the police with a detailed
description of you and the direction you
were heading in when they last saw you.

THINGS YOU CAN AFFORD TO BUY WITH YOUR STATE PENSION

About 0.5 per cent of an averagely priced new car.

About 0.12 per cent of a Jaguar XK.

About 0.000116 per cent of Jackson Pollock's painting *No. 5*, 1948.

Eight cans of paint so you can create your own Jackson Pollock *No. 5.*

One hundred and ninety-three Mars Bars – and the good news is that now you're retired you only have to 'rest and play', so these Mars Bars will go even further than they would for someone who has to 'work' as well.

THINGS YOU'LL DO DURING THE COURSE OF YOUR RETIREMENT

Trace your ancestors back to the creation of the Earth (if not before).

OH WOW! MY GREAT, GREAT, GREAT, GREAT, GREAT, GREAT, GREAT, GREAT, GREAT, GREAT, GREAT, GREAT GRANDAD WAS CALLED, 'BIG BANG'!
FAMILY TREE

Have sex two and a half times.

Learn how to tell the people who insist
on phoning you from call centres in far
flung parts of the world to 'bugger off'
in their various native tongues.

Finish the crossword *and* the sudoku every day in the newspaper.

Compare prices at six different supermarkets before buying anything.

GIVEAWAYS THAT WILL TELL PEOPLE YOU'RE RETIRED

Your car is permanently spotless.

You put your bins out mid-afternoon on the day before collection.

You read the newspaper from cover to cover every day.

BAD RETIREMENT PRESENTS THAT YOU MIGHT HAVE RECEIVED

A book called something like '1,000 Things You Must Do Before You Die' from which some wag has removed several entries to give you more of a chance of getting through them all.

A photo album of secretly taken pictures of yourself canoodling with a series of different colleagues at every work Christmas party since 1970.

Your own space in the office car park which you originally applied for about fifteen years ago.

STATISTICALLY SPEAKING – LOOKING AT YOUR WORKING LIFE

Let's say you've been working 9–5, five days a week, for roughly 45 years. That's a working life of **93,600** hours.

But you probably had around six weeks off every year for holidays and bank holidays. That's over five years gone for starters! Oh, and an hour off every day for lunch, totalling **10,350** hours.

So that means you spent around **72,450** hours of your life actually working. But did you? What about:

Sickness – At an average of 8.5 days a year that's 382 times during your working life when you phoned in and put on that sad under-the-weather voice to say you would be back as soon as you could. Total: **2,674** hours.

General chatting – A modest two ten-minute chats a day adds up to another **3,322** hours.

Cigarette breaks – Six ciggies a day, ten minutes each, there goes **9,968** hours.

Tea/coffee breaks – If you had a modest three cups a day spending ten minutes getting your drink, chatting at the machine, drinking, etc., that's **4,984** hours.

Toilet breaks – After all that tea and coffee, you will have spent at least ten minutes a day in the toilet – that's another **1,661** hours gone.

Drinking/partying – What about when it was your birthday, or when you had to take that 'client' to lunch? Let's be generous, call it a couple of hours a month, which adds up to another **1,080** hours.

General skiving – Appointments with doctors, dentists, opticians, sneaky job interviews, waiting for the gas man, moving house, getting delayed in traffic, etc., etc. Altogether probably another hour a week or **2,070** hours in total.

So, although in theory your working life totalled 45 years, in reality it was 27.2 years. That's over 17 years frittered away at your boss's expense!

And then there's all that time looking out of the window, looking up holidays, picking fluff out of your computer keyboard, rearranging the gonks on your computer…

There was probably about one hour a day when you actually did any work. It's been a tough life, hasn't it?

YOUR NEW SOCIAL CIRCLE

All the local cats' owners who tend to become unusually sociable shortly before they have to go away and need you to look after their pets.

The person behind the counter in the newsagents.

Representatives from every telephone sales team in the known universe.

HOW TO AVOID LOOKING AS THOUGH YOU'RE RETIRED

Ask the newsagent to keep your copy of
Saga Magazine under the counter.

Walk purposefully out of your house at 8 a.m. sharp every morning then creep back later in disguise.

Avoid buying the supermarket's cheap 'own-brand' products.

DRESS CODE FOR THE NEWLY-RETIRED

For him

Before lunch: pyjamas, dressing gown and slippers

After lunch: comfy jumper, expandable waistline trousers and slippers

Evening attire: any combination of the above

For her

Before lunch: expandable waistline slacks and matching pastel colour top pyjamas

After lunch: as above

Evening attire: as above with a cardy when it gets a bit nippy in the evening or with pearl necklace if entertaining

THINGS TO LOOK FORWARD TO

Your old firm offering you double your previous salary as a consultant.

Your friends retiring so you have someone to go to the pub with on a Tuesday afternoon.

Being able to eat your lunch
without any interruptions.

Being permanently on holiday.

Being able to go to the shops when they're less crowded.

Not having to pretend you're busy when the boss walks past.

THINGS IT'S LESS EASY TO LOOK FORWARD TO

Not having photocopier/Internet access at all times.

Being able to go to the shops when they're less busy but not having any money to spend.

Your spouse retiring.

YOUR NATURAL ENEMIES WILL NOW BE...

Anyone responsible for setting and administering pensions.

Anyone who starts talking about their latest fabulous pay rise

Door-to-door salesmen who now
always find you at home.

THINGS YOU CAN NOW
GET AWAY WITH

Staying up till whatever time
you damn well like.

Not changing your clothes for three days.

Eating garlic without worrying about the consequences.

Talking at length to people while they begin to look increasingly agitated because they're supposed to be back at work.

THINGS YOU CAN FEEL SMUG ABOUT

Not having to worry about redundancy.

Being able to write 'The End' at
the bottom of your CV.

HOORAY! THINGS YOU'LL NEVER HAVE TO DO AGAIN

Struggle to look your best by 7.30 a.m.

Ask when you can have your holidays.

Go to another annual appraisal
interview with your boss.

Have someone two-fifths of your age
promoted over your head so they can tell
you how to do what you've been doing
since before they were born.

THINGS YOU *THINK* YOU'LL NOW DO	THINGS YOU *WILL* NOW DO
Cruise round the Aegean	Cruise round garden centres
Walk the Pennines	Walk the dog a bit more
Get fit	Get fat
Take up a new interest	Realise you're not that interested in anything
Pursue your interest in food and wine	Pursue your interest in eating and drinking until you fall over

OPTIMUM RESULTS   PROBABLE RESULTS !

THINGS YOU WON'T QUITE BE ABLE TO GET USED TO

Realising that it's now always your turn to make the coffee.

Having no one to gossip about.

Having 24-hour access to a fridge full
of food and fighting temptation.

Not caring whether there's a
bank holiday coming up.

Having no one to discuss
last night's TV with.

If you don't do anything whatsoever, no
one's going to notice (except perhaps
for a nosy neighbour and the couple
of paramedics they call out).

THINGS YOU NEVER THOUGHT WOULD HAPPEN

You look in the mirror and realise you have started to look and dress like Victor Meldrew and/or Hyacinth Bucket.

You miss work.

You start to wonder if perhaps your boss did know what he or she was doing after all (Ha ha ha ha ha! No, but seriously…).

YOUR NEW WEEKLY HIGHLIGHTS

Going to the post office for your pension.

Staying in bed instead of queuing for your weekly train ticket.

Watching all the miserable people shuffling past your house on their way to work on Monday mornings.

'Fresh Scones Day' at the local garden centre tea room.

YOUR NEW OUTLOOK ON LIFE

You can pity the poor fools who still have to work. (Yes, them and their pathetic money and social life.)

You will be respected everywhere you go because now you're a senior citizen. (Dream on!)

At last! You're your own boss! (The trouble is you've got nothing to do.)

THINGS YOU WILL DESPERATELY TRY TO AVOID

Joining one of those afternoon clubs for the retired where you can make your own Christmas cards, toilet roll covers, place mats, boiled egg cosies, etc.

Becoming a couch potato all day as well as all evening.

Spending your entire week's pension
on a single night out.

Referring to yourself as a pensioner.

THINGS PEOPLE WILL NOW SAY TO YOU	... AND SOME HANDY ANSWERS
You must be bored out of your mind.	Only by the number of times people say that.
Do you miss work?	As often as possible.
Are you going to get a little part-time job?	What, when I've got a full-time job answering stupid questions?
What do you do all day now?	Oh, you know... Take drugs, have kinky sex and dance until dawn – unless of course it's Wednesday because that's 'Fresh Scones Day' at the local garden centre tea room.

THINGS PEOPLE WILL SAY TO AVOID ADMITTING THEY HAVE RETIRED

I'm busier than ever.

I'm a consultant.

I have been appointed emeritus
professor at the University of Life.

I'm taking 30 gap years one
after the other.

CRUEL EXPRESSIONS PEOPLE USE TO DESCRIBE BEING RETIRED

You've been placed safely beyond use.

You're waiting for your call-up papers from the graveyard.

You've been put out to pasture.

LIBERATING THINGS TO DO
NOW YOU'VE RETIRED

Smirking at the morning traffic reports
while you soak in the bath.

Smashing your alarm clock

Having breakfast and going back to bed

REASONS TO BE CHEERFUL

You can have dress-down Mondays, Tuesdays, Wednesdays and Thursdays as well as Fridays.

Your ex-boss is still having to work to help pay for your pension!

You can have breakfast in bed
every day of the week.

www.summersdale.com